ADI SANKARACHARYA

ADI SANKARACHARYA

THE VOICE OF VEDANTA

Sridevi Rao

Revised Edition

Published by
Rupa Publications India Pvt. Ltd. 2015
7/16, Ansari Road, Daryaganj
New Delhi 110002

Sales centres:
Allahabad Bengaluru Chennai
Hyderabad Jaipur Kathmandu
Kolkata Mumbai

Edition copyright © Rupa Publications India Pvt. Ltd. 2003, 2015

Text copyright © Sridevi Rao 2003, 2015

Photographs courtesy: N.R. Ramachandran,
Shankara Vidya Kendra, New Delhi, and Ajay Khullar

All rights reserved.
No part of this publication may be reproduced, transmitted,
or stored in a retrieval system, in any form or by any means, electronic,
mechanical, photocopying, recording or otherwise, without the prior
permission of the publisher.

The views and opinions expressed in this book are the author's own and
the facts are as reported by her which have been verified to the extent
possible, and the publishers are not in any way liable for the same.

ISBN: 978-81-291-3671-8

First impression 2015

10 9 8 7 6 5 4 3 2 1

The moral right of the author has been asserted.

Typeset by Ninestars Information Technologies Ltd, Chennai

Printed at : Aarvee Printers Pvt. Ltd. New Delhi

This book is sold subject to the condition that it shall not, by way
of trade or otherwise, be lent, resold, hired out, or otherwise
circulated, without the publisher's prior consent, in any form
of binding or cover other than that in which it is published.

CONTENTS

Chapter One: The Voice of Hinduism	7
Chapter Two: The Child Prodigy	12
Chapter Three: The Philosopher	26
Chapter Four: The Sage and the Son	40
Chapter Five: The Teacher and Reformer	47
Chapter Six: Architect of the Hindu Identity	62
Bibliography	70

CHAPTER ONE

THE VOICE OF HINDUISM

Adi Sankaracharya is the chief architect of the philosophical system—Vedanta, that has come to be recognised as the pre-eminent voice of Indian philosophy. At once mystical and intellectual, sublime and scholarly, covering the entire range of human experience from the empirical to the transcendental, Vedanta is one of the most complete and comprehensive philosophical systems in the world today.

This great tradition, whose genesis lay in the mystical vision of the Upanishadic seers and sages of yore, was but a feeble voice amid the clamour of the myriad religious groups that existed when Sankara was born.

Sankara lived in an age when the Vedic tradition was in decline, and when the great spiritual heritage of India—the Vedas and Upanishads, were being interpreted variously to suit the divergent beliefs of a staggering variety of sects and cults. All these groups claimed allegiance to the Vedas, though their philosophies and practices ranged from orthodox ritualism to radical atheism, from *tantric* practices that included human sacrifice to the individual practices of *puja, dana, vrata utsava* and *yatra*. This was, perhaps, inevitable because the scriptures themselves seemed to posit quite contradictory views.

Adi Sankara's radical and original reinterpretation of the scriptures, in the light of his own direct realisation of ultimate reality, succeeded in completely refurbishing them and reinstating their beauty and elegance. It also resulted in a system that unified the various Vedic sects and cults into a single stream with a common philosophical matrix. In time, this unification would evolve into the modern, homogeneous Hindu identity.

Besides refurbishing the scriptures, Sankara embarked on a highly successful mission of cleansing Vedic religious practices of their ritualistic excesses, and turning people's minds towards the core teaching of Vedanta, which is Advaita or non-dualism.

By this time, Buddhism and Jainism, which were the radical, heterodox religions that had held sway for almost a millennium, were already on the wane in India. Sankara's missionary zeal recharged and reinvigorated the Vedic religion, and brought it back to the centre-stage.

Sankara is therefore, regarded as the prime propagator of the Hindu revival movement, or renaissance of Hinduism in the country.

Sankara was a self-realised sage, brilliant philosopher and prodigious scholar; he was also, by most accounts, an extraordinary debater, a remarkable strategist, a compassionate teacher and a loving son. A charismatic figure, he was a man of the people.

It is a matter of some irony that this vibrant figure in India's spiritual heritage is also its most elusive.

10 • ADI SANKARACHARYA

Very little is known of the actual events of Sankara's life. He is known as Adi Sankaracharya or the original Sankaracharya, in order to distinguish him from his spiritual descendants who bear the same name. The biographies that were written in the couple of centuries after his death were, at best, hagiographies, with little reliable information regarding his life. For instance, it is believed that he took up *sanyasa* at the age of eight, completed his major works by the time he was sixteen and died at the age of thirty-two. Fact? One does not know. Plausible? Maybe. Even the literary works attributed to him are of questionable authorship, because it was the practice of those times for disciples to attribute their works to their guru out of a sense of reverence. Legend and fact therefore get inextricably intertwined in the life history of Sankara. For instance, stories of miraculous powers, such as his entering the body of a dead king, and improbable meetings with mythological figures, such as the meetings with the *rishi* Vyasa, abound in the traditional accounts of his life. Some of them contradict the very essence of his teachings.

Nevertheless, even without the legends, Sankara's life would stand out as one of stupendous achievement. His is a story with few parallels in the history of world philosophy.

CHAPTER TWO

THE CHILD PRODIGY

Sankara was born sometime in the eighth century, in a village on the banks of the river Purna. The village (present day Kaladi), on the banks of what is now known as river Periyar in Kerala, South India—subsisted on agriculture, and had a small population made up of different social classes.

His parents were Sivaguru and Aryamba, a prosperous, middle-aged Nambudiri Brahmin couple who had been childless for a long time. The birth of the boy was not only a joyous occasion for the couple, but also a blessed one.

Legends relate that Aryamba had performed severe penance to Lord Siva for the boon of a child. One day, the Lord appeared to her in a vision, and expressing pleasure at her deep faith and devotion to him, promised her that he would himself incarnate in the form of her first-born. It is interesting to note that Sankara's disciples, who referred to Sankara reverently as Bhagavat or Bhagavatpada, never spoke of him as being an incarnation of Siva.

Just before the birth of the child, the Lord appeared once again before the couple and asked them to choose between a child who would live a short but extraordinary life and one who would be dull, but live long and be a dutiful and devoted son to them. The couple chose the former.

Sivaguru and Aryamba now accorded the infant a welcome worthy of a god. They named him Sankara, meaning 'accomplisher of peace and good'.

From very early on, Sankara displayed signs that he was indeed a gifted child. By most accounts, he started speaking by the time he was one and was writing prolifically and intelligently by the time he was two. He was hailed as *eka-sruti-dâra*, one who can retain anything that had been read just once, and had, by the time he was three, memorised a great deal of poetry, legend and history.

His parents gave him the kind of upbringing and education accorded to boys in Nambudiri households of the time. A pious couple, Sivaguru and Aryamba performed all the rituals expected of their class, excelling especially in the growing practice of *dâna-dharma* or

14 • ADI SANKARACHARYA

giving alms to charity. Therefore, Sankara was exposed to Vedic tradition even as a boy and must have had a fine sense of the role expected of him as an adult. When he was three, his parents performed *cûdâkarman* or tonsure ceremony on him and sent him off to school to begin his formal studies.

The village school or *gurukula* would hold its lessons under the shade of a tree or in one of the two temples of the village. The language of learning and instruction was, of course, Sanskrit. The teacher was an official

appointed by the local administration. The pupils would live together, begging for alms from nearby homes for sustenance. In this humble environment, the boy, who would in later years distill a sophisticated and path-breaking philosophical system from the Vedas and Upanishads, began his study of the scriptures, grammar, rhetoric and logic. He was precociously talented and was a very quick learner. It is said he had mastered all the four Vedas (though he himself belonged to the tradition specialising in Yajurveda and was not really required to study them all) and the six *Vedangas* in just two years' time. He learned to recite extensively from the epics and *puranas*. He was introduced to the doctrines of *tarka*, *mimamsa* and *dharmasastra*. These were the fourteen branches of learning or *vidyas* that were taught at *gurukulas* of the time.

When Sankara was five years old, his parents planned to perform the *upanayana* or thread ceremony, which would, according to Brahminical tradition, formally end his childhood and mark his induction into the life of a *brahmachari*, thus making him eligible to perform the sacrificial rites prescribed in the Vedas. Sivaguru died before this ceremony could be performed, but after due interval, it was completed. The five-year-old then went back to school to complete his education before he could assume his responsibilities as head of his little family.

Tender though in age, Sankara seems to have conducted himself with rare focus and diligence. He was hungry for knowledge, and taught himself a lot more than what the village teacher could offer. Very often, wandering mendicants would pass by the village, taking up temporary residence at the village temples. Through them, Sankara acquainted himself with the complex philosophical systems of the various sects prevalent at the time.

Politically, socially and religiously, it was a time when old traditions and systems were breaking down. There was no single imperial ruler, and the political scene was one of perpetual strife among small kingdoms. The Gupta Period had come to an end, the powerful Harshavardhana had died in Kanauj, the era of Pulakesin II was over in the Deccan, and the Chera, Chola, Pandya and Pallava kingdoms exercised power more or less equally over the South.

Socially, the disintegration of old—or more precisely, Vedic traditions meant that the *varna* system of class distinctions based on profession had given way to the rigid *jati* or caste system based on heredity. Certainly, the young Sankara had identified strongly with his *jati*, and it would take a pivotal encounter with a social outcaste years later, to jolt the maturing sage out of its stultifying hold.

Religion and ritual were no longer the preserve of one class of people. The performance of sacrificial rites was still the exclusive birthright of the Brahmins, but people of all classes enthusiastically conducted *puja, vrata, dana* and *samskara*, both in their homes and in temples. The abstract philosophies of Vedic religion had long been replaced with images of gods and goddesses that people could relate to. Magic, marvel and miracle were popular, with the performance of tantric rites to invoke invisible powers being rampant. Tantric practices involving animal and even human sacrifice were not unknown. In the seventh and eighth centuries, the Bhakti Movement had swept like a tidal wave into homes and hearts, resonating to the emotionally charged devotional songs of the Alvars and Nayanmars, the poet-saints of the Tamil kingdoms.

Young Sankara absorbed it all. He also grappled intellectually with the philosophies of diverse sects, which included Jainas, Ajivakas or those who denied the existence of the individual soul, Buddhists who talked of *sunyata*, Kapilas who adhered to the dualistic Sankhya system, ritualistic Purva Mimamsakas, non-dualistic Vedantins, Pauranikas with their many gods and goddesses and Lokayatas or materialists...

By the time he was eight, Sankara was a storehouse of philosophical knowledge and was already teaching others in his little village school.

18 • ADI SANKARACHARYA

He had also, according to legend, already acquired miraculous powers. One day, on his daily round of begging for alms, the seven-year-old Sankara found himself at the doorstep of a poor Brahmin household. The man of the house was away and the lady was dismayed that there was no food to offer the young *brahmachari*. She searched high and low and finally found a gooseberry, which she gave as alms, with the blessing, 'May your self-knowledge shine like the *amalaka* (gooseberry) in one's palm.' (The gooseberry was traditionally used as a metaphor for the direct, unambiguous perception of reality. In the enlightened state, things are seen as they are, without the obstructions of thoughts, feelings, and interpretations—just as a gooseberry on one's palm is perceived as it is, with clarity and precision.) Great compassion flowed from the boy when he saw the heart of generosity in the midst of abject poverty and he spontaneously composed a poem to Goddess Lakshmi, praying for the blessings of wealth for the poor family. Immediately, there was a shower of golden gooseberries. The *Kanakadharastotra* (prayer for a rain of gold) of Sankara is traditionally believed to have been the poem composed on this occasion.

On a later occasion, he was moved by the sight of his mother having to walk a long way to the river everyday for personal and other chores. One day, the legends say, she was so exhausted that she fainted on her way back from the river. Sankara used his yoga *siddhis* to cause the river to change course and flow closer to their home, thereby relieving his mother's hardship. In the process, a little Krishna temple was submerged, and he later installed a new shrine by the river.

Sometime in his eighth year, Sankara decided that he had learned all he could from the school, so stayed home and devoted himself to performing Vedic rites as his father used to. He was a model *brahmachari*, but the years of study had instilled deep inside him an unshakeable desire for Absolute Knowledge, and he now found his thoughts turning increasingly towards living the life of a *sanyasin* in search of Truth.

Sankara, the legends say, gently revealed his feelings to his mother, but Aryamba, who doted on him, would not hear of it. He coaxed and pleaded, but in vain. And then one day while he bathed in the Purna, a crocodile sank its teeth in to his ankle. He yelled for help, and a distraught Aryamba ran hither and thither on the bank, not knowing how to save her son.

Then Sankara called out, 'Please, mother, if you want me to live, give me your permission to become a *sanyasin*.' Cornered, the helpless Aryamba agreed, and no sooner did she give her permission than the crocodile released the lad's leg. Sankara threw the sacred thread that bound him to the life of the *brahmachari* into the raging waters of the Purna and gained his release into *sanyasa*.

He donned saffron robes, picked up his alms bowl and staff, and was ready to depart. Heavy-hearted at leaving his mother alone, he made sure that relatives, who would be her heirs, would take care of her well-being. He promised Aryamba that he would be back with her at the time of her death and would perform her last rites, as any son should. For a *sanyasin* who has severed all worldly bonds and relationships this would be a sacrilegious thing to do, but the promise was made with great love and compassion—and would be kept, when the time came, regardless of strong opposition from the community.

And then he set off, first in search of a *guru* who would formally initiate him into *sanyasa* and set him on the path to liberation.

What must it have been like for the eight-year-old to leave the comfort and security of a loving home and embark on a lonely journey that would lead him he knew not where? Did he follow bands of mendicants, or tread a lonely path through the thick forests of the West Coast, or was he, as some texts say, accompanied by a fellow student and friend? From available records, we can only guess that he journeyed through the present-day Palghat, Sringeri and Gokarna, on to Onkaresvara on the banks of the Narmada, where the climactic meeting with his guru would take place.

In a secluded cave on the banks of the Narmada, lived a sage known as Govindapada. He was a great yogi and was said to have retained a youthful body despite his advanced age. Few had actually seen him or heard him, as he spent most of his time inside his cave in *samadhi*. Most importantly, he was a disciple of the great Vedantin, Gaudapada.

It was most probably for this last reason that Sankara sought Govindapada. Although he became a disciple of Govindapada, Sankara is seen as, and seems to have considered himself to be, the direct spiritual descendant of Gaudapada. It was his vision and teaching that Sankara received from Govindapada, which he then crystallised into the form in which it is known today.

Details of Gaudapada's life available to us are scanty and contradictory but most probably, he was a great learned man like his disciple Govindapada and lived well beyond a hundred years. A seer and a mystic, he related his direct experience of Realisation to the mystical sections of the Upanishads and, based on them, fashioned the genesis of a philosophical system that would find its full form and expression in the teachings of Sankara.

The key teaching of Gaudapada was Advaita, or non-duality. He identified ultimate reality with Brahman, the eternal and indescribable Absolute. The phenomenal world of duality, of subject and object, is false, but appears to be real because of *maya* or the illusive projection of the mind, he declared.

Gaudapada described the nature of Brahman and the means to it in these lines in his work:

'Manodrysyam idam dvaitam
Manaso hyamanibhave dvaitam naivopalabhyate
Na sankalpayate yada'

Which could be roughly translated as:

The world of duality is a projection of the mind.
When the mind becomes non-mind, this world of objectifications ceases to exist.
The mind becomes non-mind when it stops imagining or constructing.

Our consciousness, said Gaudapada, exists in four states: waking, sleeping, dreaming and transcendent. In the transcendental state, when thoughts have ceased and all objects dropped, the quiescent consciousness realises its oneness with Brahman. This is the state of *nirvikalpa-samadhi*.

Sankara must have been familiar with these teachings when he arrived at the cave where Govindapada sat in *samadhi*.

Many are the legends that describe the dramatic events that led to Sankara being accepted by Govindapada as pupil. Some narrate that he circumambulated the cave thrice, then beseeched Govindapada to accept him as disciple. 'Who are you?' demanded the sage. Sankara gave him his name and background. 'Who are you?' repeated the sage and this time Sankara answered that he was the manifestation of the very Self as Sankara—a truly non-dualistic reply that brought Govindapada out of his cave. Then there are the legends that say that Govindapada had been foretold of Sankara's arrival by Sage Vyasa and had been waiting for the momentous occasion.

The stories are at best apocryphal.

Govindapada initiated Sankara into *sanyasa*, transmitted to him the teachings of Advaita and guided his spiritual progress through the next three or four years. For Sankara, those years were a time of tremendous spiritual growth, deepening understanding and Realisation. He articulated these insights in a series of poems including *Narmadastaka, Pratassmarana, Sadhana-Pancaka, Yati-Pancaka, Vakyavrttii, Viveka-cudamani, Dasa-sloki*, and the philosophical treatises

Atmanatma-viveka, Ekadasottarasata-vakya-grantha, Pancikarna and *Balabodhini*.

Supremely happy about his pupil's progress, Govindapada acknowledged Sankara's spiritual maturity and his direct Realisation of the Absolute by giving him permission to write a commentary on the *Brahmasutras*. A philosophical work of no mean complexity, it would require no less than an enlightened sage to write a commentary on the *Brahmasutras*. Sankara had the spiritual stature to write that commentary, and also to be a master himself. He would, from now on, be known as Sankaracharya. He was twelve years old.

The epoch of Sankara, one of stupendous achievement and unparalleled religious zeal, was about to begin.

CHAPTER THREE

THE PHILOSOPHER

Taking leave of his teacher, Sankara proceeded to Kasi, the epicentre of religious India. Kasi was, even then, a chaotic city, a high-energy melting pot of diverse religious and sectarian practices, learning and scholarship, trade and business, cultural and secular activities. It was a city of monks and masters, ritualists and ascetics, *bhaktas* and pandits, in a volatile mix of orthodoxy and heterodoxy. It was, in short, the ideal setting for the mammoth endeavour that Sankara would immediately undertake.

The twelve-year-old Sankara settled down near the Manikarnika Ghat. Scholars and historians tell us that the next four years were a period of tremendous literary activity for Sankara. At some point he is said to have travelled to the Himalayas, to Badrinath and restored the worship of Badrinarayana at the temple there. This was the time when he wrote the major works that put forth his philosophy with dazzling clarity. Other than these literary outputs, there are no other incidents or episodes reported to have taken place at this time.

Here then is our picture of Sankara between the ages of twelve and sixteen. Fresh from his training under Govindapada, where he had come to a great Realisation, he seems to have withdrawn into the life of a recluse, absorbed in his inner life; for a while he lived in complete solitude, in the remote regions of the Upper Himalayas.

It was not as if he spent his days lost in contemplation, either. Intellectually and creatively, this was probably the richest period of his life. He related his own direct Realisation to the truths contained in the scriptures and fashioned a philosophical system that was breathtaking in its scope and content.

In later years, Sankara would rely on his own powers of analytical reasoning to refute the philosophies of other religions and sects. But now, he drew exclusively from the scriptures to establish his philosophy of Advaita. And in this he had a clear-cut purpose, which was to refurbish the Vedic texts to which he owed complete allegiance. The texts were riddled with contradictions, and had therefore become open to misinterpretations that resulted in bizarre ritualistic excesses. Sankara saw it as

his mission to reinterpret the scriptures in the light of his own Realisation, and provide an elegant framework from which their truths would ring out triumphantly, in one resoundingly clear voice.

He delved into the intricate semantics, the elaborate prosody, the dense aphorisms and the apparently self-contradictory pronouncements of the scriptures, extracted the overt and embedded truths from them and meticulously developed an integral system that would serenely accept all manner of religious practice, yet remain inviolable in the pristine revelation at its core.

In this effort, Sankara differed greatly from his equally illustrious predecessor, Gautama Buddha, who did not draw from the scriptures (with which he, too, must have been deeply familiar) in his teachings. Was it the conditioning of Sankara's orthodox Brahmin upbringing and traditional education that prompted him to give primacy to the scriptures over the realised truth of his

ADI SANKARACHARYA • 29

direct personal experience? Actually, Sankara was even here following the injunction of the scriptures. He believed, as the Upanishads declared, that complete Realisation and deep spiritual insight is facilitated by three instruments of knowledge or *pramanas*. The first *pramana* is *shruti*, or the revelations contained in the scriptures. As the Upanishads express it:

The Self, my dear, how is it to be seen? It has to be heard about first; it should be heard about from those who have studied the scriptures.

The *mahavakyas* of the scriptures, especially, could lead one to sudden and spontaneous Realisation:

Prajnami brahma—Brahman is pure consciousness
Ayamatma brahma—This Atman is Brahman
Tat tvam asi—You are that
Aham brahmasmi—I am Brahman

The second *pramana* is *yukti*, or reasoning. The mind seeks explanations and reasoning, and when that is fully satisfied, deep faith is born. This deep faith spurs the mind on the spiritual quest; longing for ultimate knowledge, completely subsumed in the inner quest, the mind suddenly comes to Realisation. This direct personal experience is the greatest and final *pramana*—*Svanubhuti*. Therefore, for Sankara, the scriptures are important; an elegant philosophical system that can stand logical scrutiny is important. But above all, is ultimate knowledge that comes only with direct experience.

And so, at the heart of Sankara's spiritual vision was the direct and luminous revelation of Brahman as the Self of all the world and all beings. It was embodied in a philosophical system that knit heterogeneous strands from his traditional, social and religious milieu and heritage, and brought the diverse sects of the time into one common fold.

Literally, Advaita means 'non-dual' or 'not-two'. The term seeks to describe the nature of ultimate reality. It seeks to articulate an answer to the spiritual quest: ultimately, what is the universe, who am I?

Our True Self or True Nature, according to Advaita, is Brahman. Ultimately, Brahman is who we truly are. Brahman is the I of Who am I. Dualistic philosophies have a theory of creation, attributing it to a divine power, Brahman, that creates matter and life alike—the I, or *Atman*, is separate from this Divine Creator. Advaita, however, proclaims the I, the *Atman*, to be Brahman—'*Aham Brahmasmi*, I am Brahman', is its central tenet. The phenomenal—world of beings and non-beings, matter and energy—is not apart from Brahman. The phenomenal world and Brahman are not-two. Neither does the phenomenal world, ultimately, become one with Brahman—it *is* Brahman.

Brahman is eternal, unmoving. It is without attributes. It neither acts, nor causes action—to use a philosophical term which led to Sankara's famed conceptualisation of *maya*, it is not even the 'first cause'; very simply, creation is not a function of Brahman.

Since Brahman alone is real, the phenomenal world, *from the standpoint of Brahman*, is unreal or an illusion. This is a core teaching of Advaita, reflected in the Upanishadic lines:

Brahma satyam, jagan mithya
Jivo Brahmaiva na parah.

To transliterate:

Brahman alone is real;
The world is illusory;
The Self and Brahman are not separate.

Sankara was not the first to arrive at this truth. Non-dualism, as a direct personal Realisation, makes up a great

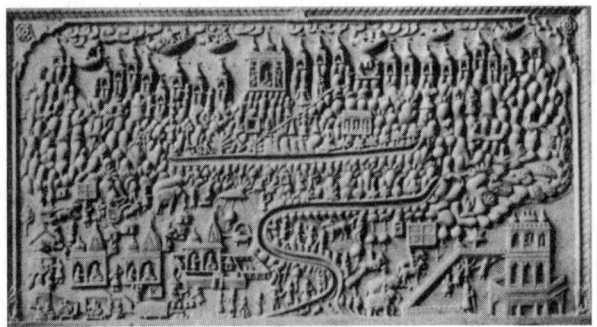

A symbolic representation of a Jain holy place.
Carved marble panel, nineteenth century

part of the mystical outpourings in the later Upanishads, and was Sankara's spiritual heritage from a great lineage of teachers who had themselves realised it directly.

Non-dualism is at the core of religions like Jainism and Buddhism, which predate Sankara by over a millennium.

Sankara's pre-eminent position as a proponent of Advaita comes from the fact that, from the Advaitic standpoint, he spun off from the scriptures a comprehensive philosophy that includes every aspect of both worldly and transcendental experience. The scriptures speak in two voices: one of dualism (which allows for the worship of Brahman, the divine creator, in the anthropomorphic forms of a plethora of gods and goddesses) and the other of the absolute monism of Advaita, which, strictly speaking, recognises no god other than the Self.

Sankara reconciled this virtual doublespeak of the scriptures by a multilayered approach to the spiritual life. While he upheld the absolute and sole reality of Brahman, he did not dismiss the experience of the phenomenal, empirical world or even the multiplicity of gods in the scriptures. Rather, he sought to create a spiritual framework within which all of human experience would have its place.

Sankara's philosophical framework was essentially made up of three levels of reality. On the first level, *paramarthika satta*, is Absolute or ultimate reality or

Brahman. This Brahman is the Self of all things; it is ever pure, free and perfect. Not subject to time, space and causation, it exists as *sat* (Absolute truth), *chit* (Absolute consciousness) and *ananda* (Absolute bliss).

On the second level, *vyavaharika satta*, is the empirical world of beings and non-beings, things and objects. It is subject to time, space and causation. The *jiva* or soul too, belongs to this level of reality. On the third level, *pratibhasika satta* (which arises from the second level), is apparent reality. This is the psychic realm of the mind, where things that have no empirical reality can still influence or trouble the mind.

How do these three levels of reality come about? If creation is not a function of Brahman that does not act, how does the phenomenal world come to be? To explain this, Sankara introduced the cornerstone of his philosophy: *maya*. In Vedic times, the term *maya* was used to denote the power of magic with which a god could make human beings believe in what turns out to be an illusion. In the Upanishads, this was extended to mean the powerful force that creates the cosmic illusion that the phenomenal world is real. For the Advaitins, *maya* is thus that cosmic force that presents the infinite Brahman or Self as the finite phenomenal world. *Maya* is reflected at the individual level by human ignorance (*avidya*) of the true divine nature of the self, which man has mistaken

for the empirical ego but which is in reality identical with Brahman.

Through *maya* also comes into being Isvara, the empirical counterpart of Brahman. Worship of Isvara, therefore, is the empirical equivalent of worship of Brahman. The levels of reality thus make space for a higher and lower Brahman: the *nirguna* Brahman, which is without attributes, and *saguna* Brahman, the lower Brahman or Isvara of the empirical world with idealised attributes, which can be worshipped through the multiplicity of gods and goddesses.

This framework made it possible for Sankara to bring the predominant and populist *Smartha-Puranic* religion of the day under the Vedantic umbrella. It also made possible a multilayered approach to ultimate Realisation that incorporated all popular modes of worship and spiritual practice.

After clearly defining the nature of reality at its many levels, Sankara's philosophy turns to its implication on the religious life and addresses the question: what is the path to liberation? Is it one of *pravrtilakshana dharma* (pursuit of moral and social good) or *nivrittilakshana dharma* (withdrawal from the material world)?

For Sankara, liberation comes with the removal of *avidya*. (Sankara sometimes used the terms *maya* and *avidya* interchangeably.) Due to ignorance, or *avidya*, we think of ourselves as separate from Brahman. When this *avidya* drops, then who or what we really are is revealed to us. We do not *become* anything, we do not move at all from any one point to another, we simply discover what we really are. In that instant of Realisation, the phenomenal world and all that we *ultimately are not* become negated or *not real.*

Brahman can only be *known* or intuited. There is no real way to liberation, no path and no practice because all practice belongs to the realm of action. Action belongs to the empirical world; it implies a movement from one state to another; it makes *becoming* possible. Liberation, however, is not to *become* Brahman (which implies that self and Brahman are at some point separate, dual) but to *know* oneself *as* Brahman. The person who has thus realised Brahman then becomes established in *jnana* (ultimate knowledge).

While the intuition of the Absolute comes suddenly and spontaneously, Sankara maintained, there are certain states of mind—the not-acting, not-thinking state that *dhyana* (meditation) leads to—that are more conducive to the arising of Self-knowledge. These states of mind can be cultivated, but the journey on this path of *jnana* (knowledge)—*jnana marga*—is an arduous one and suitable only for renunciates.

The scriptures, and especially the Bhagvad Gita, talk of the three ways or *margas* to liberation as being that of *bhakti* (devotional worship), *karma* (work or duty) and *jnana*. Yet, the Advaitic ideal of non-action, which makes the all-important distinction between *knowing* and *acting* and therefore upholds *jnana marga*, seems to negate *bhakti* or *karman* as a means to liberation.

But Sankara does find a place for these disciplines within his framework. The disinterested or detached performance of one's duties (*karman*), meditation (*dhyana*), and devotional worship (*bhakti*) are all actions that help purify the mind and ignite a desire to know the Self.

Sankara saw true *bhakti* as selfless devotion and complete surrender of the empirical self to Brahman, its goal being the ultimate Realisation of the god that is worshipped as none other than the Self. *Bhakti* towards dualistic gods and goddesses would not, strictly speaking, find a place in the Advaitic tradition, but Sankara accepted it as a rudimentary beginning along the path of liberation. Dualistic *bhakti* would lead to *mukti*, or well-being in the relative world, while *bhakti* that is a total self-surrender to Brahman that is the Self leads to *moksha* or Absolute well-being. Dualistic *bhakti*, he said, would inevitably lead one to the non-dual *bhakti* of total self-surrender. Sankara therefore saw a process that begins with desire-less action and the purification of the mind with single-pointed devotion, and culminates in the 'action-less action' of meditation, which prepares the mind so that Self-knowledge may arise.

However, *karman* and *bhakti* are relevant only as long as one remains in *avidya* or ignorance. Once there is Self-knowledge, nothing applies. The liberated *jnani* (or *jivanmukti*) transcends all *dharmas* prescribed by the scriptures, but in his actions reflects all the good qualities of detachment and compassion advocated by them.

Sankara's philosophical system is, thus, at once radical and orthodox. It was the work of pure genius—and would be the springboard from which he would launch his unifying and reformist mission.

CHAPTER FOUR

THE SAGE AND THE SON

Sankara developed his elaborate yet minutely fine-tuned philosophy of Vedanta through commentaries (*bhashyas*) on the scriptures. It is generally believed that he completed his major works by the time he was sixteen. However, it is unclear in what order the works were written.

The major works fall into three broad categories: the commentaries on the Upanishads, which contain the first glimmerings of intuitive knowledge and direct experience; a commentary on the *Brahmasutras*, which supported the revelations in the Upanishads with reason and logic to form a philosophical tradition called Vedanta; and a commentary on the *Bhagvad Gita*, which dealt with the practical implications of Vedic knowledge and philosophy.

Together, the commentaries established a system that was comprehensive and complete, covering every aspect of transcendental and spiritual/religious experience.

The most important of them is his commentary on the *Brahmasutras*. Called the *Brahmasutrabhashya*, this *magnum opus* by Sankara is considered the most sacred, complete and definitive work of Advaitic literature.

The *Brahmasutras* are generally believed to have been written by Badarayana, sometime between 600 and 200 BC. They systemised the philosophy of the later Upanishads into the form known as Vedanta. The later Upanishads had moved away from the idea of a pantheon of gods and goddesses, and put forth the idea of a single cosmic principle—the Brahman—as the true Self of all sentient beings, indeed as the matrix of the phenomenal world. It was, in fact, not just an idea but also the expression of the direct experience of the seers and mystics who composed the verses of the later Upanishads.

The Vedanta developed in the *Brahmasutras* picked up and continued this theme, interpreting it in the light of the views of great thinkers like Badari, Jaimini, Asmarathya, Atreya, Kasakrtsna and Auduloni. The personal vision of the seers was stated in abstract conceptual terms and backed by logical arguments to form a complex, sophisticated philosophical system.

The *Brahmasutras* discussed intricate ideas that were reinterpreted by Sankara in the *Brahmasutrabhashya* and that formed the core of his philosophy of Advaita.

Other than the major works, Sankara is also said to have written a series of commentaries on lesser known scriptures, and composed a few *stotras* (hymns) during this period. A large number of works, including hymns and minor philosophical treatises, are believed to have been composed by him in the next sixteen years that he spent travelling across the length and breadth of the subcontinent. The authenticity of all these works as those of Sankara has, however, been disputed by scholars and historians down the ages. At best, it may be that parts of the works were written by Sankara; many of them may well have been written by disciples and then attributed to Sankara.

The total number of literary works attributed to Sankara include twenty-three *Bhashya Granthas* (commentaries), fifty-four *Prakarana* and *Upadesha Granthas* (philosophical treatises), and seventy-six *Stotra Stuti Granthas* (hymns and verses). Of these, those recognised as the authentic works of Sankara are: the commentaries on the *Brahmasutra, Bhagvad Gita* and the ten Upanishads; the philosophical treatises *Upadesa Sahasri, Vivekachudamani, Aparoksha Anubhuti* and *Atmabodha;* the *stotras Anandalahiri, Govinda Ahtaka,*

Dakshinamurti Stotra, Dasa Sloki, Dvadasa Panjarika, Bhaja Govindam Stotra, Vishnu Shatpadi, Harimide Stotra, Kaupina Panchaka, Manishapanchaka and *Nirvana Shtaka*.

By the time he was sixteen, Sankara was thus a deeply enlightened sage and unmatched scholar. Yet some vestiges of his Brahmin upbringing remained, and would now be challenged in one of the most dramatic and moving episodes to be recorded about his life.

It is an encounter that has acquired mythical dimensions in the hands of Sankara's hagiographers—quite unnecessarily so, for shorn of the myths, what we see is a man of great courage, who dared to repudiate the staunch orthodoxy of his upbringing and social milieu in the face of truth.

One day, Sankara was walking down to the Ganga with his disciples when he saw a *chandala*, a social outcaste, walking up the path with his dogs. Instinctively, the sixteen-year-old called out to him to move aside and make way for him and his disciples.

The *chandala* stood his ground and issued a challenge that would become a great learning experience in the young sage's life. The lines ascribed to him are rather long, but the gist of his questions to Sankara went like this:

'You preach that the Vedas teach the non-dual Brahman to be the only reality and that it is immutable and never polluted. If this is so, how has this sense of difference overtaken you?'

'You asked me to move aside and make way for you. To whom were your words addressed, O Learned Sir? To the body, which comes from the same source and performs the same functions in the case of both a Brahmin and a social outcaste? Or to the Atman, the witnessing Consciousness, which is the same in all, unaffected by the body?'

'How do differences such as, "This is a Brahmin, this is a social outcaste" arise in non-dual experience?'

'Forgetting... one's own true nature as the Spirit—beyond thought and words, unmanifest, beginningless, endless and pure—how have you come to identify yourself with your body?'

'If you say that your conduct is meant only for the guidance of the world, even then how can you explain such conduct in the light of non-dualistic experience?'

Instantly, Sankara awoke to the truth underlying the words and, freed from the last vestiges of dualistic thinking, sang a moving verse—the *Manishapanchakam*—in praise of Siva as the Self. Mythology narrates that the *chandala* revealed himself to be Lord Siva, and the dogs—the four Vedas. Philosophically interpreted, the encounter ended with Sankara expressing the deep

Realisation that the *chandala*, like all beings, could not be anything other than Siva.

Sometime after he turned sixteen, it is believed, Sankara intuited that his mother was dying. This is another powerful episode that presents us Sankara the

The Spatika Linga

man, full of love and compassion, breaking the shackles of an orthodox tradition.

By most accounts, Sankara reached his mother's side before she died. He is said to have composed the *Tattvabodha* and *Krsnastaka* as a final spiritual instruction for his dying mother. After her death, he wanted to fulfill the promise made to her when he left home, and perform the last rites himself. It was unheard of for a *sanyasin* to do so, and the orthodox Nambudiris of the village refused to go along with it. But Sankara paid no heed. Unable to carry the body by himself, he cut it up into pieces, which he then carried to a pyre that he had built in the corner of the garden, and consigned them to flames.

CHAPTER FIVE

THE TEACHER AND REFORMER

There is a legend about Sankara that relates that he was destined to live a short life, but was twice granted extensions of his lifespan by *rishis*.

Even before his birth, say the legends, Sankara's parents had been told that their son would have a short life. He was, in fact, destined to live only up to the age of eight. Just before he turned eight, however, a group of sages is said to have visited their home, and pleased with Aryamba's devotion and Sankara's knowledge, had blessed him by doubling his lifespan.

When he was sixteen, and had just completed writing his major commentaries, the great *rishi* Vyasa is said to have visited him and engaged him in a lengthy debate over the scriptures. Pleased with the depth of understanding Sankara displayed during the debate, the *rishi*, too, blessed him by further doubling his lifespan.

Scholars and historians present a more rational basis for this probable sectioning of Sankara's life in the three distinct phases that he went through. The first phase, till age eight, was the childhood period. The second phase, from eight to sixteen was a period of inner work, during which he gained his spiritual insights under the

tutelage of Govindapada and then went on to develop his philosophical system through his writings. The third phase, from age sixteen to his death at thirty-two, was that of Sankara as the wandering mendicant and missionary.

In this last phase, we see a picture of Sankara quite different from the brooding young man of intellectual intensity of the earlier phases. Now we see a Sankara of indefatigable action, travelling and teaching tirelessly through the length and breadth of the subcontinent not once, but thrice. He travelled by foot, with a small band of devotees, probably wearing just his saffron robe and wooden sandals, with his only possessions, the *kamandali* (begging bowl) and *danda* (walking stick) of the *sanyasin*, and living on whatever alms they received each day.

During this period, scores of disciples came to him, some of them accompanying him wherever he went. Among them, four were destined to become the torchbearers of Sankara's great teachings. When each of them first met him is not known, but how they came to be his disciples is described dramatically in the legends.

One day, while Sankara was in Kasi, a young Brahmin called Visnusarma sought him as a teacher. Visnusarma hailed from the Chola Kingdom in South India and had searched far and wide for a teacher. Attracted to the boy-sage, he begged to be accepted as disciple. Sankara initiated him into *sanyasa* and gave him the name Sanandana.

Others followed, and soon Sankara was surrounded by disciples wherever he went.

The disciples, say the legends, revered their master, but Sanandana was the most devoted of them all. He easily outshone the others, but not understanding why this was so, the disciples began to feel that the *acharya* himself was playing favourites, giving special attention to Sanandana. Intuiting the mood, Sankara decided to show them the simplicity and incandescent purity of Sanandana's devotion that set him apart from the rest.

One day, while Sankara was bathing in the Ganga with his disciples, he noticed Sanandana on the opposite bank. He called out to Sanandana to come. Instantly, Sanandana turned in the direction of his master's voice and started walking. Unaware of where he was placing his feet, his mind and heart fixed single-pointedly on his master, he took the shortest path to the beloved figure— across the waters of the Ganga. A lotus flower bloomed under every footfall, supporting him across the river.

From then on, Sanandana came to be known as *Padmapada*, the lotus-footed one.

Sankara's meeting with Mandana Mishra is generally given great importance, possibly because it is in this instance that the *acharya* seems to have revealed best his incredible intellectual prowess and debating skills. Sankara had not actually set out to meet him—he had, in fact, sought Mandana's teacher, the renowned Purva Mimamsa scholar and philosopher Kumarila Bhatta, to engage him in debate.

Purva Mimamsa was the most prevalent religious sect of the time. The dualistic Purva Mimamsa school believed that the way to salvation lay in the strict observance of all the rituals prescribed in the Vedas. The foremost proponent of this school was Kumarila, who had won renown by defeating the Buddhists in philosophical debate. Sankara knew that he needed to either win over Kumarila or defeat him in debate if the Advaita teachings were to be accepted by the masses and survive his lifetime.

By the time Sankara reached Prayaga (present-day Allahabad), where Kumarila lived, the latter had already accepted the truths of Advaita. In fact, Sankara arrived to find Kumarila in the act of immolating himself in excruciatingly slow degree by immersing himself in a pit of slow-burning paddy husk. He was doing this to expiate two sins he considered himself to have committed. One was that of his studying Buddhism under the false identity of a Buddhist monk so that he could learn their doctrines and decimate them later in debate. The second sin was that of his spurning of Isvara to put his faith in Purva Mimamsa.

Quite the strategist, Sankara quickly requested him to write a *vrattika* on his *Brahmasutrabhashya*. Kumarila, however, directed him to his student Mandana Mishra, whose scholastic abilities equalled that of his teacher.

Sankara hastened to Mandana, and defeated him in a series of fiery debates held over a few days. The legends give a dramatic and colourful account of the happenings of those days.

When Sankara arrived at the home of Mandana, the legends relate, it was closed from inside as Mandana was busy performing a *shraddha* ceremony. Sankara, however, used his yogic powers and entered the house. Mandana was furious when he saw Sankara, because it was believed to be inauspicious for a *sanyasin* who has renounced all rituals to be present during such ceremonies.

A verbal duel is said to have followed, at the end of which Mandana agreed to debate with Sankara. He also agreed to embrace Advaita and take up *sanyasa* if Sankara was able to defeat him in the debate. Mandana's wife Ubhaya Bharati, no mean scholar herself, was asked to be the referee. Busy with household duties, Ubhaya Bharati doubted that she would have the time to sit through the debates. So before they commenced, she placed a garland around their necks—the wearer of the garland that faded first, she declared, would be the loser.

The debate raged on for days. At every mid-day, Ubhaya Bharati would interrupt—to invite the *grihastha* Mandana for lunch and *sanyasin* Sankara for *bhiksha* (alms). Then one day she invited both of them for *bhiksha*—signifying that Mandana had lost the debate. Simultaneously, the garland around his neck began to fade and wither while Sankara's remained fresh.

Sankara initiated Mandana into *sanyasa* and gave him the name Sureshvara. One of Sankara's most ardent disciples, Sureshvara would, after Sankara's death, head the Sankara *mutt* at Sringeri.

When Sankara was visiting a town referred to as Sri Bali, in South India, he was approached by a man named Prabhakara, who had a son who behaved strangely—not quite retarded, but not very sanely either. Prabhakara wanted to know if the *acharya* could help him in any way. The boy seemed to be lost to the world, but when Sankara gently asked him why he behaved like an inert being, he burst into a song. The twelve-verse discourse on the nature of Atman ended with the refrain: 'I am the Self that is of the nature of eternal consciousness.' Sankara accepted him as a disciple, initiated him into *sanyasa* and gave him the name Hasthamalaka.

While Sankara was at Sringeri, Kalanatha, a young man of no learning, begged to be his personal attendant. He would wait on the *acharya* hand and foot, and when he gave his discourses to his pupils, would stand a little away from the group, drinking in every word his master uttered. One day, it is said, the disciples ridiculed Kalanatha as a dull-witted person. Suddenly, Kalanatha sang a hymn, composed in the difficult *totaka* metre, in praise of Sankara. From then on, he was accepted as one of the disciples and was known as Totakacharya.

Sankara, though very young, clearly had a paternalistic relationship with his disciples. He openly displayed his deep affection, concern and care for them. The disciples revered him but felt confident enough to question him and even confront him. There is an incident between the *acharya* and Padmapada that reflects the close and loving bond between master and disciple.

Sankara stayed for a while in Sringeri (in present-day Karnataka) with his disciples. While there, he commissioned Padmapada and Sureshvara to write commentaries on his works. It is said that after completing the task, Padmapada wanted to go on a pilgrimage on his own. Sankara at first said no. The proximity of the guru, he said, is the real place of pilgrimage, and the ablutions of the guru's feet the real *tirtha* (holy water). Travel would only cause distraction, he tried telling Padmapada; he would spend all his time worrying about food and shelter rather than perceiving the Atman, which is best done through the instructions of the guru.

But Padmapada was determined. He put up an impressive argument, saying that conveniences are hardly conducive to spiritual attainment, and inconveniences, disease and death have to be faced. At this, Sankara exclaimed that he had only been testing his acolyte's determination and gave him permission to go. And then, by most accounts, he fussed over his favourite disciple, sending him off with words of caution and advice: 'Do not stay too long in any place; take known and well-used paths; don't travel in the dark; don't trust strangers too much.'

If the first part of Sankara's mission was the refurbishing of the Vedas and the restoration of Vedanta to its rightful place, the second part seems to have been the reformation of the religious practices of the time and the popularisation of Vedanta.

As a religious reformer, Sankara was a man of the people, a charismatic figure who won the hearts of those who came into contact with him. He spoke to people in the terms that they understood; he visited their temples and participated in their worship. He sang moving hymns and songs soaked in the flavour of *bhakti*, while he gently tried to turn their mind towards the ideal of Advaita.

He travelled to as many places as he could, however far-flung, in order to meet people of as many sects as possible. No historical record of his itinerary is available, but from the legends surrounding various temples, it can be surmised that he criss-crossed the country, from Puri in the east to Gokarna in the west; from Rameswaram in the south to Kashmir in the north. He visited Srisailam, Mookambika, Sri Bali, Sringeri, Kanchipuram, Vidarbha, Ujjain, Badrinath and Kedarnath, among others.

Sri Chakra

In all the temples he visited, Sankara introduced various reforms in the methods of worship. He rid Vedic rituals of their degenerate practices and excesses, and ushered a simplicity and purity of heartfelt worship in temples and in homes. He sang the praises of the deities in beautiful hymns, including *Dakshinamurti stotram, Devyaparadhakshamapana stotram, Shivananandalahiri* and others.

There is some ambiguity about Sankara's stand on *tantric* practices. During Sankara's time, the deity of the Kamakshi temple in Kanchipuram was that of the Devi in her fearsome aspect. It is believed that Sankara drew the Sri Chakra *yantra* and performed an elaborate ritual worship to invoke the goddess in her benign, peaceful aspect. He is also believed to have visited the Sarada temple in Kashmir and worshipped the deity there as a consort of the supreme god, again with the drawing of the Sri Chakra *yantra*. He is believed to have composed one of his best-known hymns, the beautiful *Saundaryalahiri* in praise of the Devi, here. These incidents seem to indicate that he actively supported the worship of Shakti.

In his social ideas, however, Sankara was somewhat orthodox. He upheld the Vedic practice of dividing society into four classes or *varnas* based on profession, but his frequent bemoaning of the dismal state of society as it existed then seems to indicate that he was unhappy with the rigid *jati* system that had become prevalent. Even the distinctions of the *varna* system, he believed, were operative only as long as one remained ignorant of the Self. When the Self is Realised, all social identities, obligations and distinctions cease to exist. Self Realisation, he believed, could happen spontaneously to anyone, irrespective of *jati*—it would be possible for a *Sudra* to become a *jnani* or a Realised being. *Jati* did not also matter to the follower of *jnana marga*, who would, in Sankara's system, necessarily have to be a renunciate, a *sanyasin*; but if one was not on the path of renunciation, the studying of the scriptures was important before he entered the last, meditative phase of his life, and such scriptural studies, Sankara did believe, was possible only for the Brahmin.

Sankara also believed in the efficacy of the *varnashramadharma*—the four stages of life as delineated by the Vedas. First was the stage of childhood; then came youth or *brahmacharya,* a period of purity, celibacy and studying of scriptures; then *grihasthya*

60 • ADI SANKARACHARYA

An artistic sculpture at Sri Vidyashankara Temple in Sringeri

fulfilling family and social obligations as a householder; and finally, *vanaprastha*, the severing of worldly ties and turning the mind inward.

The mix of orthodoxy and heterodoxy in Sankara's teachings had a far-reaching, reformist impact on the religious milieu. But coming as it did centuries after the radical, reformist social stands taken by Buddhism and Jainism, its impact on the social milieu was rather limited.

CHAPTER SIX

ARCHITECT OF THE HINDU IDENTITY

At every place he visited, Sankara would debate with the local heads and scholars of the prevalent religious sects. The establishment of a school of philosophy by refuting the premises of others in debate was an accepted practice of the day. The debates were not so much for public entertainment as for the fine-tuning of painstakingly synthesised philosophies. Refuting the doctrines of a rival sect was part of this process of plugging all the loopholes in one's system—the more you debated, therefore, the more polished your approach and the more complete your synthesis became. In the skill of debate, Sankara, by all accounts, was simply brilliant. He debated with Sankhya enthusiasts, Purva Mimamsakas, Buddhists, Jainas, Pasupatas, Vaishnavas,

Maheshvaras, Kapalikas many others. He is not known to have lost a single debate.

However, Sankara's aim was clearly not to 'defeat' or decimate any particular sect but to guide its adherents onto the path of Advaita, while finding a place for their beliefs and practices in his broad philosophical framework of Vedanta. For instance, Sankara had accommodated many of the premises of the complex dualistic Sankhya system—especially its cosmology—in his philosophy. Buddhism was the one religion he trenchantly opposed, although it was one he came closest to in terms of ultimate truth or vision. However, being aware of the mood of the times, he appropriated a principal teaching of that religion, that of non-violence to all sentient beings, as being of Vedic origin.

But the crucial factor in his acceptance by the vast majority was his absorption of *bhakti* at its many levels within the Vedantic fold. It was a time when the *smartha-puranic* sect, which worshipped the myriad gods and goddesses of Vedic mythology, held sway. The Bhakti Movement, spearheaded by the Alvars and Nayanmars, had drawn together worshippers of Vedic, folk and tribal gods and goddesses alike in a single devotional stream. By finding a place, however basic, for this dualistic *bhakti* in his framework, Sankara was able to extend his influence over every such sect of the day. He regrouped

64 • ADI SANKARACHARYA

them into six broad categories, according to the deities predominantly worshipped: Vaishnava (Vishnu), Shaiva (Shiva), Sakta (Shakti), Saura (Surya), Ganapatya (Ganapati) and Kaumara (Skandha or Kumara). He came to be regarded as *Sanmatasthaspanacharya*—the founder of the Six Sects.

Till then, each sect had functioned as an independent religious group, the only commonality among the sects being the Vedic or *puranic* origin of their mythologies and deities. By grouping them thus and bringing them under the common Vedantic umbrella, Sankara gave them not only a common origin but also a common

Adi Sankara drew inspiration for setting up the first matha on watching this sight—a serpent giving shade to a pregnant frog

religious/philosophical matrix. The diverse sects now began to assume a common identity. Over the centuries, this nascent identity would evolve to form the modern Hindu identity.

Sankara was keen to establish, within the Vedantic tradition, a monastic order on the lines of the highly efficient Buddhist ones. The *mathas*, or monastic centres, would also serve the spiritual needs of the community. He established four such *mathas*, one in each geographical region, and designated his four chief disciples to head them—Hasthamalaka headed Govardhana Matha at Puri in the east, Sureshvara headed Sarada Matha at Sringeri in the south, Padmapada headed Kalika Matha at Dwarka in the west and Totakacharya headed Jyothir Matha near Badrinath in the north. There is some controversy over whether he established the one at Kanchipuram, where he apparently stayed for a while and where he ceremonially ascended the *Sarvajnapitha* or Seat of Omniscience.

During the time of Sankara, there were numerous wandering mendicants who belonged to no particular order. Sankara grouped them into ten different orders of the Vedantic tradition, giving them a monastic 'family' and access to residential facilities, studies and spiritual guidance.

66 • ADI SANKARACHARYA

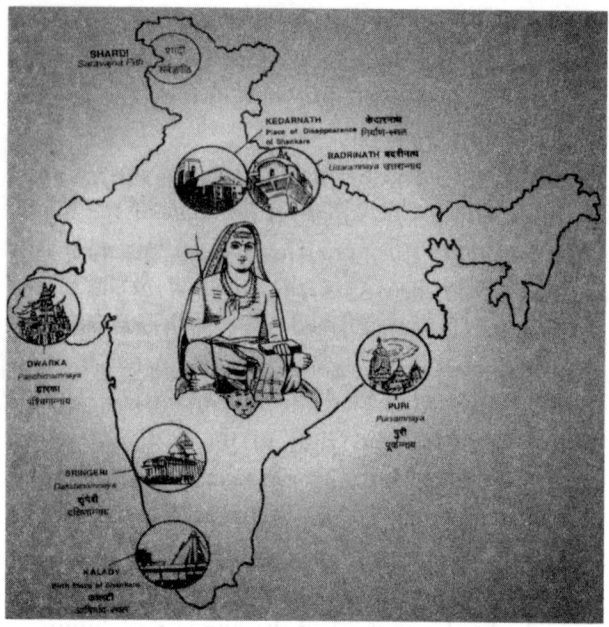

There is a tract authored by Sankara, called *Mahanusasana*, where he gives tips and pointers to his disciples and the members of the monastic orders that he founded. He advised them not to confine themselves to one place but to wander constantly to preach the truth of Advaita and inculcate right conduct (more specifically, the *varnashramadharma*) among people. It is reflective of the kind of life he led in his last years—travelling, preaching, teaching and reforming, ceaselessly and tirelessly.

When did he meet his end? And where?

Unfortunately, or maybe appropriately for a man whose life events are subsumed in the effulgence of his teachings, this is unknown. There are different claims made by different sets of people regarding the place of his *samadhi*, as to whether his life ended in the Himalayas, near Kedarnath, in Kashmir or in Kanchipuram. The generally accepted view is that he ended his earthly life in Kedarnath. He was, by most accounts, thirty-two years old when he died.

The Badrinarayan Temple at Badrinath

The Vedantic tradition of Sankara has continued to flourish in India till today. Modern sages like Ramana Maharshi who, like Sankara, came to spontaneous and direct Realisation, found validation for their vision in his Advaitic teachings. Pre-eminent philosophers like Vivekananda, S. Radhakrishnan and Sri Aurobindo based their teachings on Vedanta, and sought to extend its truths into the realms of ethics, history, religion, cosmology and evolution. Ritualistic and dualistic modes of worship continue to be followed within the Hindu tradition to this day. However, with the eclecticism of more modern times, Advaitic practices like *dhyana* are increasingly being followed by people outside the monastic order.

And so, in the midst of the colour and clamour of the Hindu practices, the voice of Sankara still comes, almost unbidden—in the form of questions that visit our hearts

Sri Aurobindo   *Vivekananda*   *Sri Ramana Maharshi*

and minds. When, after all the energy and zeal of our worship and rituals are spent, we turn, for a moment, inward: What, ultimately, is reality? Who, ultimately, am I?

It is in that moment that our journey into Sankara's vision could begin.

BIBLIOGRAPHY

An Interpretation of the Life & Teachings of Shri Shankaracharya (*Elucidatory & Reconciliatory*) by Swami Mukhyananda, Sri Ramakrishna Advaita Ashrama, 1998, Ernakulam

Shankaracharya by T S Rukmani, Publications Division, Ministry of Information and Broadcasting, Government of India, March 1994, New Delhi

Life and Thought of Sankaracharya by Govind Chandra Pande, Motilal Banarsidass Publishers, 1994, New Delhi

Sankara Digvijaya—The Traditional Life of Sri Sankaracharya by Madhava Vidyaranya, Translated by Swami Tapasyananda, Sri Ramakrishna Math, Chennai

Indian Philosophy—Volume II by Dr S. Radhakrishnan, Macmillan New York; George Allen & Unwin Ltd, London, 1940

Sankaracharya by T.M.P Mahadevan, National Book Trust, India, New Delhi, 1968